Lean Foundation and

Lean Processes

by Vo Thi Minh Nhut and Nguyen Van Thanh Tien

Legal Disclaimer:
The information contained in this book and its contents is not designed to
replace any form of medical or professional advice; and is not meant to
replace the need for independent medical, financial, legal, or other
professional advice or services that may be required. The content and
information in this book have been provided for educational and
entertainment purposes only.

The content and information contained in this book have been compiled
from sources deemed reliable, and they are accurate to the best of the
Author's knowledge, information, and belief. However, the Author cannot
guarantee its accuracy and validity and therefore cannot be held liable for
any errors and/or omissions. Further, changes are periodically made to this
book as needed. Where appropriate and/or necessary, you must consult a
professional (including but not limited to your doctor, attorney, financial
advisor, or other such professional) before using any of the suggested
remedies, techniques, and/or information in this book.

Upon using this book's contents and information, you agree to hold
harmless the Author from any damages, costs, and expenses, including any
legal fees potentially resulting from the application of any of the
information in this book. This disclaimer applies to any loss, damages, or
injury caused by the use and application of this book's contents, whether
directly or indirectly, whether for breach of contract, tort, negligence,
personal injury, criminal intent, or under any other circumstance.

You agree to accept all risks of using the information presented in this
book.

You agree that by continuing to read this book, where appropriate and/or
necessary, you shall consult a professional (including but not limited to your
doctor, attorney, financial advisor, or other such professional) before using
any of the suggested remedies, techniques, or information in this book..

Contents

First Words

In today's business climate, every company is focused on serving their customers at the lowest possible cost, and that's what lean practices are all about. In a lean company, they works hard to eliminate waste, reduce costs, improve quality and increase speed throughout all their business processes. And that's what this course is all about. In this book, we'll cover lean practices and how they are used in a continuous improvement culture. We'll explore how lean principles are applied to processes in both the manufacturing and service sectors. And finally, we'll examine the importance of applying lean thinking throughout your organization. If that's what you're looking for, you're in the right place.

Chapter 1. Basic Foundation on Lean

1. What is lean?

Everyone is talking about lean. And no, I don't mean the latest diet or fitness trend. Everywhere I look companies are exploring on how they can apply lean principles to their business processes, whether they're a manufacturing company or a service provider. But what is lean? Before we apply this concept let's define what it is and understand the four basic goals of lean. Lean is all about the process, or I should say processes since lean principles and tools can be applied to every process in every business. Like production processes on a factory floor or standard processes used in restaurants or the processes to admit a patient into the hospital. Simply put, lean is about efficiency, moving material, information, and ideas through a process in a smooth, well organized manner while removing waste and decreasing costs along the way.

Lean is a set of tools and applications that allow us to do just that.

To define the concept itself, we can find that **lean has four basic goals.**

The first goal is to eliminate waste. Waste is defined as any part of the process that does not add value for the customer. Your job is to review a process with the goal of eliminating any non value added step. This streamlines the process and increases its efficiency. Examples of eliminating waste include reducing waiting time at service centers, decreasing transportation distances for faster delivery, or eliminating scrap in production processes. The second goal is to reduce cost. Nowadays it seems that nothing is emphasized more than cost reduction, and certainly anything you can do to eliminate waste in your processes will help you to reduce costs. But you can go beyond this by thinking about processes as part of a bigger system.

Providing your customers with an internet link to track their package shipment can eliminate the need for call center personnel. Offering more ATM machines can reduce the number of bank tellers needed. Having the customer place their order at the counter allows restaurants to reduce their wait staff. All of these provide sufficient low cost options to more expensive customer service systems. The third goal is to improve quality. Quality is at the heart of lean. For processes to become smooth and efficient machines must be properly maintained. Incoming materials must be defect free and service staff must be exceptionally well trained. Products and processes must be designed properly to ensure quality output. I think you can see that reaching and maintaining high levels of quality is very closely connected to eliminating waste and reducing costs. Lastly the fourth goal is to increase speed and response times. Lean is all about being quick, efficient, and highly responsive to customer needs. Lean companies are fast to design and release new products to the marketplace, to deliver on time every time, and to answer customer inquiries. All of this depends heavily on every aspect of company operations working together as one system. To understand lean you must recognize that these four principles operate in step with each other. In effect, they're equal parts of one integrated system. These four basic goals of lean, eliminating waste, reducing costs, improving quality, and increasing speed, lay the foundation for how you can use lean operating tools to improve performance in your organization.

2. Why use lean?

Lean is not a program, it is a total strategy. Alex Miller said that. He's a professor of management at the University of Tennessee, and he's often quoted on lean manufacturing practices. When most people think of lean, they think of the Toyota tools and techniques that streamline processes and eliminate waste and improve quality at the source. They think of the tactics of lean at the shop floor or office level. But Professor Miller is right.

As a corporate approach, a strategy or philosophy for the entire organization, a mindset for every employee, we must start effective lean program at the very top of the company. That's what drives a company to implement those lean practices and apply lean tactics at its operational levels. That's what determines why you should use lean. A strong lean strategy focuses on two very important aspects of your business, your competitors and your customers.

First, your competitors become more challenging every day. You know that your organization must continuously improve to meet and beat that competition. You can't stand still while everyone else is moving forward. A recent study by a global manufacturing magazine revealed the top ten lean manufacturers in the world. As you would suspect, Toyota ranked number one. It's interesting to note that the other nine companies are US-based corporations, and names that you'd probably recognize, like Intel and Nike and Ford. These are examples of some of the strongest businesses in the world. Lean is implemented by the best and most competitive companies as a corporate strategy and lean practices is being integrating throughout their organization all around the world. To keep up with or better yet, to stay ahead of that level of competition, whether you manufacture products or provide services for your customers, you need a strong lean program, one that starts at the top.

Second, you must consider that your customers become

more demanding every day. Everyone seems to want more features at less cost. Lean helps you to meet your demanding customers' needs. Lean allows you to eliminate waste, reduce unnecessary steps, deliver perfect orders, be on time and be cost competitive. And that's the way you can meet your customer's expectations every time. And that's exactly what your customer expects from you. Every one of these top ten companies is known for being very proactive in meeting their customers' expectations. From start to finish, lean focuses on the customer. Regardless of the role you play in your company, ask yourself can lean help me to serve my customers better? Can lean help me be more competitive? I bet you'll find the answer to be a resounding yes.

3. Continuous Improvement

- I saw a cartoon recently on the lean.org website. It perfectly described the continuous improvement approach through the eyes of a Lean philosophy. First, you see the classic scene of the optimist smiling at the glass half full then you see the pessimist frowning at the glass half empty. In the final scene, the Lean thinker is wondering why the glass is twice as big as it needs to be. He's thinking about how he can make that glass even better than it is right now. He's thinking about how he can redesign that glass so that half of it is not wasted.

Lean thinking drives continuous improvement and the Lean technique that drives continuous improvement throughout the organization is Kaizen. Kaizen which is a Japanese term calls for small incremental improvements that are continuously made over the long-term.

Kaizen is intended to be a pervasive mindset in which all employees are continuously looking for better ways of doing their job as they go about their workday. We see examples of Kaizen activities throughout the organization as design engineers review new materials, line workers eliminate wasted steps and delivery drivers find more efficient routes but it's not just about making the improvements. It's also the attitude that anything can be made better. A Lean thinker believes that it can always be better no matter how good it is right now. For Kaizen to be effective, it's important that employees are empowered to make changes.

It is a must that each person have a channel to make recommendations that are heard by the organization or if appropriate, the authority to implement the change directly but sometimes a problem comes up that is both critical and immediate. This is a tact to a Kaizen event, sometimes called the Kaizen Blitz. It's a major project, very intense and executed very quickly. Lots of resources, people, materials and money are dedicated to solving the problem and fixing the process immediately. Today, every organization recognizes the need for continuous improvement but that's not always been the case. For many years, American companies operated under the belief that if it isn't broke, don't fix it. That just doesn't work anymore. Global competition and increasingly more demanding customers caused companies to look for more and more ways to reduce their costs and cost reduction drives the company to look for ways to improve every aspect of their operations. Continuous improvement has become a key part of corporate culture in successful organizations. Reviewing standard business processes is always a good place to start. Most processes where they're designed to make products or to provide services were designed quickly at the very beginning and unfortunately, they were never updated. I've seen factories making products with the same recipes and specifications that were created during the prototype stage. A continuous improvement mindset propelled by the Kaizen approach will drive a continuous review of processes, practices and procedures and not just for the manufacturing areas. Early on, one of the biggest misconceptions of Lean was that it was for manufacturing only. Lean and its continuous improvement mindset is for everyone and you practice it daily by applying a Kaizen approach to your job. How about your processes? Take a look at something you do every day. Even if it isn't broke, can you fix it?

Chapter 2. Lean Processes

1. Process mapping

- Have you ever wanted to simplify a process, but didn't know where to begin? You know this process can be improved, but you're not sure exactly where. Or perhaps someone is trying to describe a process to you, and you just don't get it. If you want to understand a process, it's a good idea to start by drawing a picture.

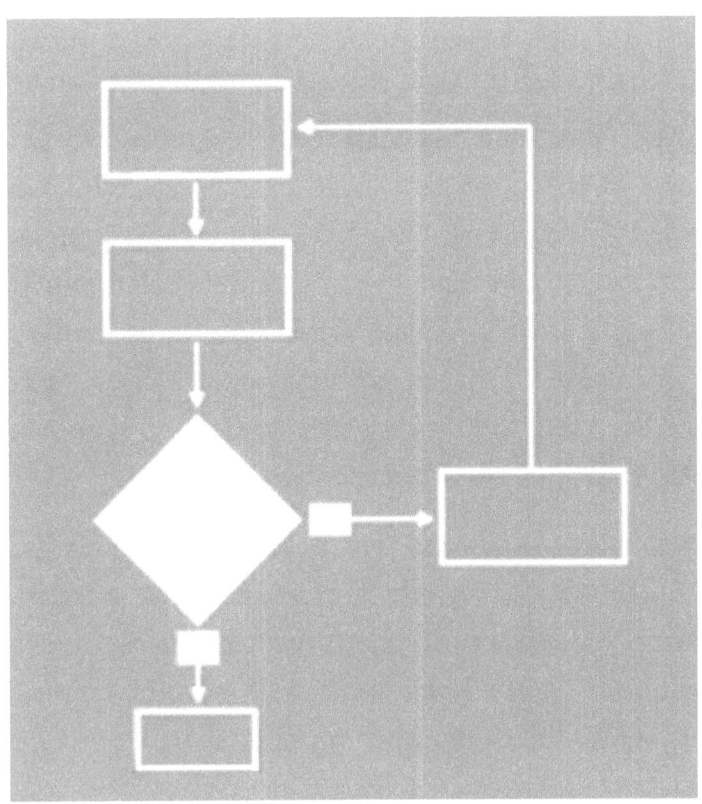

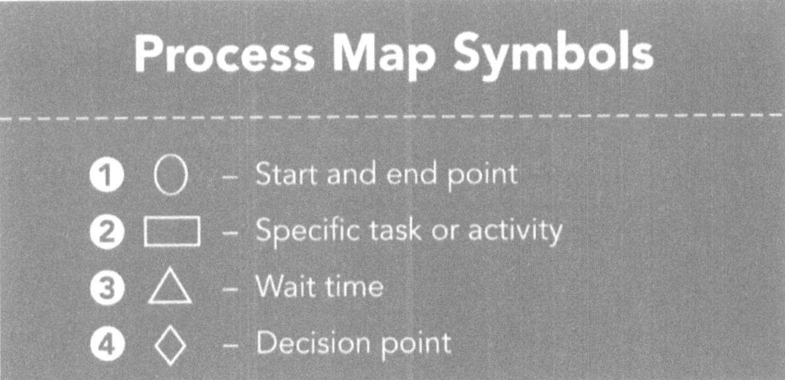

This is called a process map and it's the first step in business process improvement. A process map

13

identifies the sequence of activities in that process, or the flow of materials, or the flow of information within the process. Drawing a process diagram forces you to focus on the boundaries of the process. Where does it start? Where does it end? What activities are included in the process, and equally important, what is not part of the process? I realize this may sound rather simplistic, but these answers are critical to your success in understanding the process. There are two basic components of a process.

First, there are tasks, which are the specific jobs that when sequenced correctly, create the final output of the process. And second, there are activities, which are a group of tasks that create some intermediate output. When drawing a process map, there are five basic symbols you need to know. When you put these together in the proper sequence, you have a detailed explanation of your process.

First is an oval, which tells you the starting point and the ending point of the process.

Second, a rectangle, which denotes a specific task or activity that contributes to the process.

Third is a triangle, which indicates waiting. As we all know, just about every process has some waiting time. Whether it's material waiting for an available machine in the factory or a truck waiting to be loaded at the warehouse or a customer waiting in the drive-through line at McDonald's. There's always some waiting time, it seems. Fourth is a diamond, which denotes a decision point. Based on the decision, the process will continue in one direction or another. And last is an arrow, which indicates the direction of travel or flow. So, a very basic process map, one that is drawn at the macro level, would look something like this. This simple diagram could be a high-level map of the process used when getting a haircut or having the oil changed in your car. A map of the haircut process would look like this. And that's an important point I want you to remember. Start with a large-scale map and then fill in the details as required to produce the exact process map you need.

This simple approach keeps you from getting bogged down in too many details at the beginning. Start simple and then dig deeper. With a map of the process, you are now ready to understand and to improve your process. And that's what process mapping is all about. You want to understand your process in sufficient detail, which allows you to find areas for possible improvement. Try this out. Pick a process from your work that you're interested in or you want to understand better or you want to improve. Or maybe a process from your personal life or your home life that you think could be done better. Draw a picture using these basic symbols and components, then use your diagram to explain the process to someone else. Someone who's not already familiar with the process. I'm sure you'll agree, that if you want to understand a process, start by drawing a picture.

2. Value stream analysis

Now, that's a terrific quote from Bruce Hamilton who's the president of a consulting company that specializes in Lean Six Sigma. For sure, this is a guy who knows something about process improvement. Value stream analysis is all about improving your processes, removing those things that get in the way of your work. Most of us call these non-value added steps. One excellent tool for value steam analysis is the Lean Improvement Cycle, a five step process developed by the Lean

Enterprise Institute but before we discuss this process, let's talk about two very important considerations. **First, you must remember to start with the customer and end with the customer.** Your process is designed to meet a specific customer need and this determines what you should improve. **Second, you must always keep in mind the Seven Wastes of Lean.**

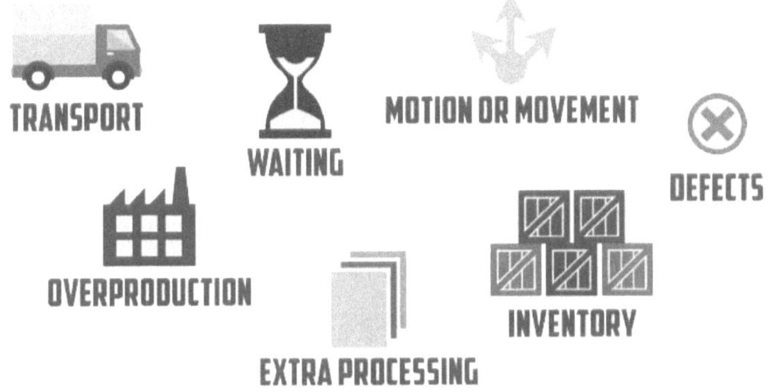

The first waste is unnecessary transportation of people and parts between processes. For example, having suppliers located close to your factory can decrease transportation efforts. Excessive inventory is a waste not just because of the increased cost but because extra inventory tends to hide other operational problems like quality issues. The third waste is unnecessary motion within a process. Organizing each workstation helps reduce this waste. The waste of waiting is probably the most serious and gets the most attention in a factory setting. For example, work in process might have to wait at a key operation because of excessive inventory levels or because of machine breakdown. The fifth waste is over-processing which ties directly back to your customer needs. Engineering tolerances for example should meet your customers' expectations but not exceed them. The waste of overproduction means that you are making too many products or making products before they're needed to meet demand. This is often caused by producing in large batches or by having products that take a long time to complete. The last of our seven wastes is defects. Every defective item you make creates more cost, additional work and customer complaints. You can't completely eliminate the seven wastes. Your goal is to remove any unnecessary amount in each of these categories. For example, you'll always have waiting time but you should work to reduce it to the lowest level possible.

Now, let's get to that five step Lean Improvement Cycle.

Step one is to define value from the perspective of the customer. If we apply this to a manufacturing company, this actually defines the product you'll make. What are your customers' expectations? What will your customer pay for and equally important, what will they not pay for?

Step two is to map the value stream. Now that you have defined your product, draw a process diagram in detail showing all the task and activities that deliver that product to your customer then work to eliminate all non-value added steps in the process guided by your customer's definition of value in step one. You now have a streamlined version of what it takes to make and deliver your product.

Step three is to create the flow that most efficiently makes that delivery. Here is where you try to tighten your process by attacking those seven areas of potential waste. For example, you might be able to shorten some delivery transportation distances or reduce some process waiting times.

Step four is to establish pull as an approach where possible. Allow customer demand to pull your product or service through the process increasing speed and response times. For example, in a factory operating purely with the pull approach, you would not start materials until you have a customer order for the final product.

Step five is to seek perfection. Begin again continuously improving the process until all waste is removed. All steps are streamlined and perfect value is delivered to your customer. Vince Lombardi, the great American football coach, believed that you can never reach perfection but if you strive for perfection, you can achieve excellence.

The five step Lean Improvement Cycle with a continuous emphasis on the customer and eliminating waste is a very effective tool for value stream analysis. This tool can be applied to your products, your services and to your individual processes with equal success. At this moment, maybe you're thinking about a troublesome process or a specific customer issue. Why not try this approach to improving your business process right now?

With your customer in mind, start at step one.

3. Process reengineering

Process maps are terrific, providing a great vehicle to better understand our processes and to sort through the details in search of opportunities for improvement. But sometimes it helps to take a more holistic view of the process. You can look at standardizing key processes across the organization for example, allowing consistency of quality and output. You can look at technology to improve overall company performance, like implementing new software for major activities.

Focusing on energy consumption, or seeking suggestions from shop floor employees are also excellent holistic approaches to process improvement. But sometimes you should go beyond that. Sometimes you should consider redesigning or restructuring or remodeling the process itself. This is where Business Process Re-Engineering comes in. Business Process Re-Engineering asks you to rethink the way you are doing your work to help you better serve your customers needs.

I read an article several years ago from the organization BP Trends which outlined a very nice four step model for doing just that. It's a pretty basic diagram that looks something like this.

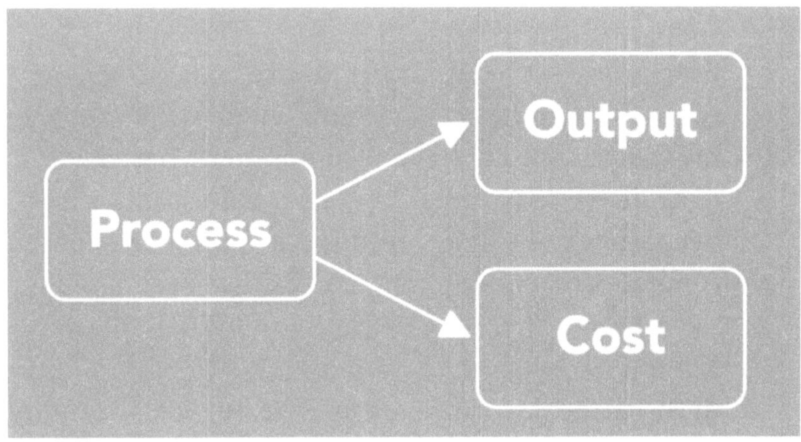

This diagram helps you to view the process from a higher more aggregated level. Your focus is on the outcomes of the process. What is the result, and what does it cost to produce that result rather than the detailed steps of the process. With this diagram in mind, you can develop your model with four straightforward steps.

Step one is to describe the process.

Basically, what product or service are you providing for your customer? You don't need a process map for this step, you just need to understand what the product or service is. For example, my process might be to produce notebook computers. I color this box green because a process is a good thing to have since it produces output that can be sold to customers.

Step two is to determine the output of the process. I can measure this in any number of ways. For example, my output could be 200 computers per day, or 5,000 computers per week. I also color this box green because when that output is sold to customers it generates revenue for my company.

Step three is to determine costs. This can also be measured in many ways. At first you may want to take a total cost perspective and then break down cost as needed. For example, I can just state that my costs are

$500 per computer. I color this box red because of course, costs are a bad thing.

Step four is where the real work begins. How can I re-engineer this process? I bet the first thought that comes to your mind is can I decrease cost while maintaining the same level of output? Of course. It seems like every day in every way you're encouraged to find opportunities for cost reduction. Maybe you're coming up with some other ideas right now. Or maybe you're thinking, can I increase output while holding cost at the same level? I'm sure the boss would like that one, also. Or even better, you may be thinking, can I increase output and decrease cost at the same time? Everyone would approve of that idea. This four step model for process re-engineering can help you to improve your company's performance in managing output, controlling cost, and meeting customer expectations. It can help you discover if a total redesign of your process is needed. Why not try it out? Pick a key product, or even a key customer and the product they buy from you. Go into the level of detail needed to truly analyze this situation. Start with output and cost. You may discover other ways this model can improve your key business processes.

4. The principle of ideality

You've heard this in just about every problem solving median at work. Your boss says he needs everyone to

think outside the box.

Challenging problems need innovative solutions, right? I love this quote from the author Deepak Chopra. Who said, "Instead of thinking outside the box, get rid of the box". Sometimes to truly understand your business process, that's exactly what you must do. Let me introduce you to the principle of ideality. Which I discovered some time ago from the BPTrends organization. The principle of ideality states that, "The most ideal solution is one that "does not exist or, for the most part, "one that does not exist now." The ideal solution is one that is accepted without barriers. To describe this principle, I'll use a car as an example, and I'll ask myself **three simple questions.**

First, what's the purpose of a car? And what does someone use a car for? Well, many of us use our cars to go shopping or to travel to and from work or to visit with our friends or some other types of entertainment. **Second, what are the costs of owning a car?** These are all the costs of travel by car. For example, the car payment, insurance, maintenance, and gas. Not to mention the cost of the environment of automobile emissions.

The third question is very straight forward. How can I provide the primary functions of a car without the cost of travel? A straight forward question but not an easy one. Maybe it will help if I draw a picture of this process. So the question is can I shop, work, and visit with my friends without the cost of travel? The answer, of course, is yes. But I must think outside the box or perhaps even throw the box away. The more ideal car is called the internet.

Now here's what I think is the real value of this principle and looking at your competition, it might be a good idea to look at other industries. Do you think camera companies like Canon and Nikon considered cellphones as a competitor 20 years ago? Today smartphones take higher quality pictures than the professional photographer cameras of only a decade ago. Do you think car manufacturers today are considering the internet as a competitor? Okay, I don't really believe that your computer will replace your car anytime soon but consider this. The more you shop and work and visit on your computer, the less you use your car. The less you use your car, the less often you need to replace it. A consumer shift to the internet can certainly mean lower revenues for automobile makers as car sales slow down. Not to mention the impact on tire companies and the people who produce auto parts. The principle of ideality can and should be used to help your organization think without the box so to speak. Maybe you have a product that is worth thinking about right now.

5. The elegant solution

> "Customers don't want products
> and services, they want solutions
> to problems... And when it comes
> to solutions, simple is better."
>
> **– Matthew E. May**

That quote is from Matthew E. May, an advisor to the University of Toyota, and the author of a terrific book titled, The Elegant Solution. Mr. May goes on to say that elegant is even better than simple. An elegant solution is one in which the optimal outcome is reached with the least amount of effort. In other words, with the simplest approach to getting the job done. Toyota's view of simplicity is at the heart of lean practices and principles. Elegant solutions solve the problem without creating other problems that must be solved. Toyota applies this view of elegance in everything they do, but elegance is best illustrated in their approach to innovation and innovative products.

Toyota concentrates on continuous improvements in small incremental steps; the concept of Kaizen, rather than looking for that ah-hah moment of breakthrough innovation. For example, the company spent 45 years of continuous improvement efforts before entering the luxury car market with the Lexus brand, but Lexus passed up BMW and Mercedes very quickly, and in only ten years became the leading luxury brand in the U.S. market. As David Neelman, the founder of JetBlue said...

> "Innovation is trying to figure out a way to do something better than it's ever been done before."
>
> **– David Neeleman**

Lexus demonstrates this quite well. To succeed consistently over the long term, require solid procedures, and the discipline to stick to those procedures every time. Toyota's approached elegance and innovation follows three principles passed down from Sakichi Toyoda, the founder of the company that would later become Toyota motor company.

The first principle is ingenuity in craft. Toyota believes that innovation is an individual responsibility. Each person is called upon to use their expertise to constantly drive towards a better way of doing things. Again, the goal of continuous improvement. Today, most companies bring such experts together in cross-functional teams to find better methods for getting the job done.

The second principle is the pursuit of perfection, which is also everyone's job. At Toyota, imperfection drives innovation. Chasing perfection creates new products, and new ways of doing things, and Toyota has established methods to convert individual ideas into big opportunities. Following this lead, many U.S. companies today have incentive programs to reward employees for their suggestions to improve the organization.

The third principle is the rhythm of fit. A great innovation fits into the larger system, and equally important, it's a fit to the times. An often cited example of this is the introduction of iTunes to deliver individual songs to consumers. It was a perfect fit to the marketplace at the perfect time. Within the lean system at Toyota, these three principles create a path to allow elegant solutions, solutions that achieve the optimal outcome with a minimum of effort, solutions that solve problems, and create innovative ideas with the simplest approach. What guides innovation in your organization? Perhaps it would be good to take a closer look at the elegant solution.

6. The cost of complexity

"Simplicity is the ultimate sophistication." A profound statement from Leonardo da Vinci that has stood the test of time. Nowadays we would say "less is more." If I take the position that simpler is better, you are certainly aligned with the principles of Lean. For one thing, complexity drives cost within the organization. For example, the Pareto Principle indicates that 20% of your products generate 80% of your revenues, so a complex product portfolio not only drives up product cost, but increases cost for such things as inventory, raw materials, and packaging, and also drives the complexity and cost found in your customer base and your markets and the organizational structure needed to support them. On the other hand, too few products in your portfolio can mean lost opportunities and lost sales. On a continuum between simplicity and complexity, where's the right place for your business to be? That's not an easy question to answer. I turned to Michael L. George for some advice here. He's a well-known consultant on Lean Six Sigma who's written several books on the subject. A few years ago Mr. George wrote a book on Conquering Complexity in Your Business. It caught my attention the minute it was released. He provides three rules for complexity, using the beginnings of the U.S. auto industry as an example. Along the way, he discloses the cost of having too much complexity and the value of having some complexity in your business.

Rule one states that you should eliminate complexity customers will not pay for. Henry Ford, in the early stages of Ford Motor Company, serves as an excellent example. Ford was competing against horse-drawn carriages when he introduced the Model T. Driven by the need to hold down his cost, he offered one type of car in one color, black. A very simple product to match his equally simple competition. Introducing this new technology, he targeted his market with a very basic product.

Rule two states that you should exploit the complexity customers will pay for. Along came Alfred Sloan who felt that some people would pay extra for a more luxurious car offered in different colors with some additional features, and General Motors was born. It's interesting to note that in the beginning, these two companies were not competitors at all, they each targeted a different customer.

Rule three states that you should minimize costs of the complexity you offer. This holds true today, of course. To add value for your customer, operate as efficiently as possible. Continuously lower the cost of complexity. George went on to say that in any given market there's only room for one very low cost operator. I guess everyone will agree Walmart's a good example of that. It seems the only way to compete in this arena is to totally conquer it. However, there is room in each market for companies that offer customer-driven complexity, complexity that adds value in the eyes of the customer. For example, Trader Joe's and their low price, name brand items. So, between simplicity and complexity, where's the right place to be? Offer products and services demanded by your customers and give them the best value for their money.

Where do you think your company lies on this spectrum? Can you apply these principles to your organization within the company? The strategies, principles, and practices of Lean can certainly help move you in the right direction.

7. The theory of constraints

For most business organizations the goal is to maximize throughput, thereby maximizing cash flow. This is a quote from Eliyahu Goldratt and is true in delivering physical products to your customer as well as providing services: "Every aspect of how businesses do business comes down to this one objective, maximize throughput". Let's look at a definition of throughput at three different levels.

First at the company level, throughput is the rate at which you are generating cash by selling your products.

Second at the factory level, throughput is the rate at which you are making those products that you sell.

And **third at the equipment level**, throughput is the rate at which the individual machine is producing output to help make those products that you're selling. In his now famous book, The Goal, Eliyahu Goldratt took the principle of maximizing throughput down to the factory and equipment levels with his theory of constraints.

The theory of constraints proposes to maximize factory throughput by efficiently managing the bottlenecks, the machines that are constraining or limiting throughput. The belief is that anything that limits production throughput is a constraint to the system. It could be a low capacity machine or a poorly trained machine operator or a supplier with consistently late material deliveries. Another important consideration is that most systems, especially factory systems, have more than one bottleneck. In a large factory there may be several machines with a very similar capacity. In a small factory there may be several workstations with only one machine. In both examples each of these would constrain the factory's throughput. So the goal is to manage the bottlenecks in a manner that will maximize their throughput in spite of their limitations. This is why utilization is the key.

For example, you would carefully manage a low capacity machine so that it never runs out of inventory to process. Or you would carefully manage a single machine workstation so that maintenance is performed with minimal downtime. Many managers believe that you either operate your factory using the theory of constraints or you apply lean principles or perhaps employ some other tool or technique. But these concepts are not mutually exclusive.

You do not have to choose one or the other. Many lean practices are very compatible with the theory of constraints and even supportive of bottleneck management concepts. Here are some examples. Plants that follow the visual factory principle by installing lights to indicate current bottlenecks or potential bottlenecks in the system. Machines that are down for maintenance are marked as a bottleneck with a red light.

Machines with low inventories are marked as potential bottlenecks with a yellow light. Kanban cards can be used to move material between workstations on an as needed basis.

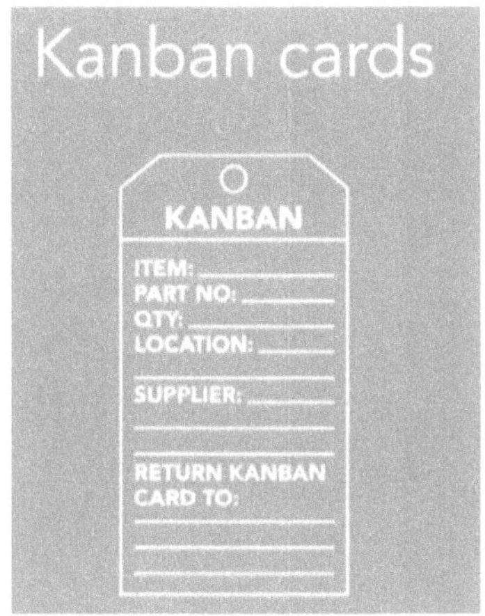

This supports the theory of constraints concept of reducing work in process inventory. Also just in time concepts support bottleneck management by bringing material to the factory, moving inventory between workstations, and delivering products to the customers only when they are needed. Both views consider inventory control as the key to success. The theory of constraints eliminates excess inventory by managing flow through the bottleneck.

Lean supports the notion of maintaining inventory at the lowest possible level. These approaches are well matched. The best companies today recognize that lean practices are very compatible with theory of constraint principles and that they can and should be used together. Take a look at your organization. Whether you're making a product or providing a service find ways to make sure you are using the best of both worlds.